S0-BLK-948

WITHDRAWN

With the
compliments
of the
Canada Council

Avec les
hommages
du Conseil des
Arts du Canada

3/16/77

HOLLANDSONG

MARVYNE JENOFF

HOLLANDSONG

AN OBERON BOOK

I

POEM FOR SILENCE AND A NAME

This poem is because
a silent man named Holland
speaks to me.

I say, and mean it,
Go away, Holland, I'm making you a surprise.

I'm not here, he says,
I'm just passing by —

that's what Holland says to me
as he leaves his hand
on my hair.

PEARS

Pears are the gentlest thing,
I challenge Holland,
hold two over his head ;

not so easily led on
he points out
some never get soft,
says Holland,
some are like North Americans—
fat bellies, little heads,
and he reaches up my belly for a pear.

I bite in and in—
pears can make gentle
even us North Americans,

pears, walnuts, coffee,
pears.

GOOD THINGS

I persuade you into sleep
for early-morning promises
and now lie smiling beside you,

my hand back-bent still touching
rides with your body's breathing,
lift and rest,
that soothes the pampered places,
the warm and naked places,
and the old broken places,

soothes and invites me but my hand is
trapped in yours, the slightest waking breaks
all heaven loose upon us—

you know it, breathing there,
I know it, smiling to the wall.

Husband it seems
what we do most is
wake the morning,

clock in our dreams,
sun in the window and our touch, these
print my soul for the day.

Evenings with minds
wild or tired we
putter,
slow for the night,

but mornings in their fresh
coincidences print the soul.

MARCH SEVENTH MORNING

On his way out
he moved our plant
into the sunshine
of the largest window

there's my man at work now,
showing them what he can do.

ARRIVING BEFORE TIME

Seven in the morning
before time
I'm the only one in the world
feet up in the best seat
on top of the building remembering
breakfast with you.

Birds are here, but they remember
other things—they hop, they fly—

stretching up here after breakfast
the only one in the world is
you and I.

THE CARROT POEM

Sometimes Holland must think
I do it all for poems—

I watch him over the salad
till he sees me, then I laugh and laugh and
rush right through him for a pencil,

well, it is all for poems,
and if not for poems there would be
carrots and parsley
with Holland's name
all over.

I take his plate
he says Aye,
I bring the teapot
he says Aye, darling—

that really speaks to me
and he responds
to how I pour the tea,

at which electric moment

I leave the poor man out and start a poem—

when he finds
something more resigned to think about
I write that down, too.

NIGHTS

Now we have a baby

I hear her cry upstairs
where neighbours live

I hear her nights
when Holland works away

Other nights she cries
we help each other
talk of other things

PORTRAIT

Holland with his soft hair
sits in the purple robe with circles, sits
up on the edge of the rocking chair,
all evening painting
brown and blue

Bach and the sometime plash of Holland's brush
in brown-blue water
are my sounds, I doze or watch him

lift his large
hand to his hair soft salt and cinnamon,
or scratch
a purple circle

His brown pipe
mutes the air

I curl around him
dozing, watching

Here comes Holland
my way
singing

He says he never sings —
if I stop him in the middle
he will call it
something else,

elusive man,

even his watching me,
he wouldn't call that singing
either

Honey
soft in his throat,
that's me

Jesus Honey,
that's me, too,
deep in his throat

Now the moon bleeds me
thick and more, the season
in its great and narrow fluctuation
like a found tide
cradles

How fast the volumes stand, telling
horribly of blood
or drily,
that do not consider the full
colours, aubergine and berry-brown,
that my new clothing
chooses

Chronicling deadlocked
nations they deny

whole provinces of scarlet
where I bloom, I bleed,
our own locked confrontation
the more ancient

THE POTTER'S MORNING

1

waking I remember
bowls
then careful fearful touching
you before waking

2

off centre
off centre
beats
whatever I hear beating
before waking

3

mornings
there is clay
mornings with you
there is also clay

The spider knows
his centre

Like a sure
compass he paces
out the bounds of his decided
universe, remembering
which side of him is
centre

Narrowing in he fastens
often
back to the centre where he
rests or plots, he doesn't
know about
mistakes,

our spider sleeping
tight round his centre
though the thunder
blow

GREENSONG

Everything is green that
has to be, the light says
go and the little car finds its
gear-shift from between us, starts just
so

Eggplant bouncing in the back ex-
cuse for a seat, seven cheese
textures for our week — home to
prick the sausage, dabble in teas,
spring refrigerated rolls against the
kitchen sink, sing

home,
even in a city day, let
everything that loves be
green

Our loving leaves the little car named
Arthur after my father, leaves his
space a field of daisies.

BALLAD FOR THE AGEING

When I was one-and-thirty
and thirty-eight was he
at the edge of the world we met and kissed
with curiosity

For all the times we'd ventured there
to see or not to see,
we kissed again and talked a day,
returned less separately

Today he proudly wears my many-
coloured tapestry,
I kiss the purple circle
and he encircles me

Now all you thirty-seven-year-olds
and twenty-nines to be,
take heart, and meet the edge of the world
with curiosity

For we warmed a purple circle,
hid it there for you to free,
when I was one-and-thirty,
and thirty-eight was he

Oh, de wif wiffle de hubband,
de wif wiffle de hubband,
de wif wiffle de hubband,
and de hubband hubble de wif.

Crumpet-toasting time again
with ginger for de hubband,
wif-tummack, hubband-tummack,
cocoa-happy all de day

Mumbly hubband, nipply wif,
playin' a came o' grib,
fifteen-four, eleventy-leven,
libble, nubble, all de day

Oh de hubband and de wif,
hub and wiffle all de day,
mumbly hubband, nipply wif,
hub and wiffle all de day

Wif find de hubband-belly,
hubband find de tit,
pigeon find de pigeon-place,
coo and libble all de day

Oh, de lubband and de fif
lub and fiffle all de day,
lub and fiffle,
fub and liffle,
hub and wiffle all de day

CATS

"Nothin' worse than sleepin' with a
  cat," he mumbles

    I get rid of my kleenex, roll right back,
    "What about wifs?"

"Ten minutes on the bed and they're up
  stretchin', washin' their faces…"

    "What about wifs?"

"blowin' their noses…"

    I scratch my teeth on his shoulder

"damn cats never lay still."

Hubband in de
kitchen under de
avocado
plant, rain
plink, summer
peep, rain
pitter, summer
plump, rain
plash, wif
plibble de hubband under de
avocado
plant.

So this is what couples do
at home
on Sunday afternoon—

I used to get
quite far around the world
on Sundays, used to be quite
pleased with myself

before I knew
you and me
at home

SUNDAY EVENING-HIS AND MINE

Blindness in the shower
is our relief—we kiss
the whole day's wine from one another's lips, kiss
soap, with slippery laughing language
and my hair between us,

your embrace around and round me makes my standing stretch,
stretch to reach our noses,
slipping laughery language,

my both hands soapy
hold you whole
in live relief

ISSUES

People like us they flatter—
where there is no choice they try to sell us
moods already painted on the walls, sell
where the only vacancy looks out,
north,
on the parking lot.

For the size and quiet we agree, the issue being
price and geographical
coincidence,

and find advantages—on the north balcony our garden
thrives, trees soften the parking lot, indoors
new things out-influence the walls,

and not the least of these is
health and humour together—chance is
good to us, we plant another petunia and agree
we might have chosen here,

but the plain issue is

where people like us
confront the winter from depends
on someone else's
transfer, marriage, death or fear
of winter.

MOVING UP

Moving up and outward
overwhelms us, we've approached
too quickly ; speculating from the new midsummer
balcony we've bought
with great bravado

seas of carpet
not enough curtains
chairs for too many guests, losing
in our panic
why we began at all ;

the huge new sofa
topples the room with its black
weight, moves in a changing
gravity as we rearrange
and finally give up on balance, unpack
little things,

our thousand
books to the ceiling
dusted one by one,
they get us back in scale.

THE NEW KITCHEN

From seed the new beginnings
open
tingle
butterfly the air

and the little carrot swells
down and round,
the root-hairs feel
into the damp dark, the root-beats carry
out the clay pot with its pores
down the wooden table
into the floor and round,

the tiny carrot
fierce in its pot
rings the whole kitchen, rings
the whole yellow kitchen
round

THE NEW BATHROOM

Whoever cleaned so conscientiously after herself
still lingers

five showers together have not made the room smell
unintruded — we long for
only our own non-perfumes,
diarrhea

Q-tips in the cabinet a week
and where the mirrors slide
dark bits of face-powder,
almost my mother's colour, still

cling,
but the day comes when we know in our hands how far
will flush the toilet, stop
the bathtub drip,

and wearied of arranging we're all set to forget it out
on the town

I pick up my false tooth from the edge of the sink
without thinking,
and we don't need her any more.

TRAINS STOP

Trains stop
everything but lawnmowers,
which have the same
effect

Both devastate—our quarrel
neither won nor lost, my savage answer
waits,
dies in the air between us

Waiting
destroys, like coming
closer

Trains stop everything but
holding

SILENCE FOR TRAINS

They stop us, signals
dinging, gradually
approach then rush at leisure past the balcony,
slow our conversation to a
silence for trains, for what makes people
go away in a long direction

Once you rode the rods
(rod-rider, rider of rods),
before my vocabulary
or beyond it, but

"Down with boxcars," you now
proclaim, fist in the air,
"Everything out where I can see it
from the balcony," and sit back
satisfied

We recreate
old childhood engines, young,
younger, laugh, push,
puff at one another, safe and
high on the balcony, our voices

over the next
train that pulls away old days alone, old
silence for what makes people
go away

BIRCH RIVER IS ALSO A PLACE

Birch River is no ordinary place
with scheduled flights per day
to book and then take
lightly –

in the same journey's time we've reached
Jerusalem and Honolulu searched and pampered,
but Birch River we must plan for by ourselves,
choose, savour the journey ;

as we approach through weather and slow change more
people begin to know about
Birch River,

but having arrived we find no
ads to tell us what to do

except Drink Coke –
we knew that all along

but must begin
somewhere

BACKS OF HOUSES

Toward the tracks we build our
backs of houses,
brick, high
windows of the children's rooms
that are not eyes—

the houses look out
onto a street made greener, after nature,
and the houses, as in friendship,
face each other
and the children who once wished for trains
play round and round the houses,
sleep, curled this way and that,
against the trains.

Below the children's windows is the place
to suntan with a magazine,
trains too far to see our
faces, people with ordinary bodies suntan
safely, or in the same oblivion
barbecue,

digest in the dusk by the embers of the grill,
enjoy the
trees this side of the tracks where the train winks through,
and talk about dentists,
barbecues,
children out of mind for the night,
train schedules,
or let the evening in the hourly
rhythm of trains be
lulled,

but for the children's
claims, which we discount
and they insist,
and the tracks one day on their tide of earth

half-inch in
closer to the backs of houses,
trees shift, too,
and the straight lines of
fences—part of the fence
buckles, falls away, and we take
notice when the picnic table begins to
rock, or the children's swings,
their windows—

one day trains make us
scatter to higher ground and
wait,
speculate about insurance,
look for our pictures in the paper, make us
seriously plan
backing farther away, both

eyes on the train. We've had to
contemplate its black or golden colour, or agree
where to fork-stick it behind the head—

and it has lasted long enough,
and the wave of earth
also weary this time round
subsides
and the bricks of houses, high
windows, faraway backyard
furniture fall back in place

like a film run finally
backward
that has looped, stopped
long enough.

TRAVELING

Traveling alone has become
traveling without you :

there I am in my old red
alone-and-chic-on-the-plane pantsuit,
long scarf and beads designed for motion,
there I am looking around the train less desperately
interested now, my clothes less
soft than I feel, weight the same but much less
likely to topple

salesmen stop me, I no longer
play their charm, my old quips come
with less conviction, less at stake—I buy
well, for our comfort

my old friend dentist disappoints me, talks of
getting away on Friday,
hurts a little,
congratulates but asks no further

I suppose things matter less,
with you I'm coming home to,
but I'm less witty, stoic, philosophical these days
and it's a whole long
hour on the silent train
home to
hold you about it.

SMALL THINGS

My mumbly man, he makes me
come in close

There I am all ready to
shout from the hill, when I spot him
crouching and his mood

cloaks me, quiets my
packages, draws me in
close, he
mumbles to his cupped
hands

and when we are all
small enough
he opens the young jay's
secret two blue
feathers, fuddled
head beginning to point,

then lifts it, reach becoming
high as the safest
part of the tree

and up there we are

The hill becomes less
high or steep,
and less beyond
his mumble,
my ear

When July
forgets itself, it's enough to

scare you in,
a cold day like that
at eight in the morning

it's enough to get the
saltshaker
in off the balcony, also the
library books, canned
nuts and the largest
ashtray, off

into the lamplight
like a stuffy evening,
sweaters and hot
tea,

and there emerges my great northern
man,
pink, bedwrinkled,
raring to jump off the balcony into the ocean
just like that

it's enough to
scare you
in

PIPE

Holland with pipe—he makes
the whole world take
its time—

our morning curtain
swells with the sun, so wafts
the aromatic world, soft
in and gentle out,

and after breakfasting, my
legs in his lap,
toe on his belly of kippers,
the world with us waits on the balcony
for trains,
dark coffee cooling—

Holland's summer
pipe—a sure
sign of the times

The universe is
better together—I'd give up
arguments to keep it
happy, how it's
changed me

Our whole year
together and there are still
streets nearby I haven't seen on foot—
you safely
ill and comfortable this
evening, my health
craves like the old days
and I prowl

at twilight, find
cut-wood smells and petunias, small
windows lit through ivy

Buttoned up and mumbling to myself
it is almost like the old days
when I used to have to walk much longer, carry
shopping bags or books, disguised as
going someplace and thinking about it

but this year with you,
the universe inside me, all is
softer
safer,

as much of it as I can
muster,

dogs and cars so suddenly
close

It turns by
pausing, by not
needing any more,

and is it the August
turning or the town—

spring weather like this and
all of Port Credit is out
short-sleeved for the breeze,
new by the river
thinking it's wonderful

but in the crux of August
out becomes
more desperately away
and the wished-for weather
hovers
bright and silent
over the sparse parking lot
and the three boys whose next year promises
something entirely different, three
boys with a bicycle in the shade
of the library

and you and I
taking in the month and town
have read much of the weekend on the quiet
balcony, strolled with ice cream
over the bridge,
stopped by the lake for
sounds, not for its far
shores. We have made our

peace, you and I, are
turning,
August after August now descending on us
like a slow
scale on the piano—

our this summer softly
lets itself go
in crickets

II

BALLAD

The balcony's blooming
it's morning it's May
peach jam for the toast
and the tea's on its way

Red roses blue violets
once I loved you
now sugar now lemon
what one word could do

The tea's in the pot
and the knife's in the tea
the cat's in the fire
you're not listening to me

Yes no I guess so
whatever you say
it's June it's September
I left yesterday

Springtime this time round seeks out
old people

in our angle of balconies brings out the
planting-fingers of the blind,
the broken-shouldered,
over the railing airs their
bedding and the light, non-existent
fluff blown free

no longer touches me
unwarmed and watching,

does not grace
our balcony of boxes and old teapots separately
planted—you one morning,
I another—we have not watered faithfully
or quarreled.

Spring on our balcony has freed
another space to pass each other in—

at night we still sit out together,
enduring the old peaceful habit, this year's
noisier neighbours sparing us
with their antics
silence to decide to speak—

sometimes I have been silent for five
seasons, weary of love's old
poems and now the balcony garden
planted with the names of flowers.

AT LOVE

Now at love we meet
suspicious,
sniff both sides,

go to it, tear it, won't let
go but into a wary
beast-sleep

Evolution is a
questionable fairy, in our sleep
flickers the once-wide daisy
smile but hovers too
a more sophisticated

vacuum, waking we claw with
sarcasm, or innocently whistle
taunting songs

Childhoods dry us, offering
summer and winter through the wheels of
other people's other business, touching
when necessary, letting us go still

groping with the other leg for
carnivals, the usual movies,
nicer people's houses, more
compatible seasons, foot-

hold, hand-hold, wholly
embracing we have somehow freed
into the same space
last year's love,
you and I

held now in a spring not warm nor cold enough,
old childhoods under separate hiding places
claim us

and there is something about touching we do not
remember,

who once encouraged tulips and now put them
in their place,

I with two crayons, you
also on the balcony
waiting for birds

Night train through the window *sees me*
sweeping spiders off the basement floor —

I never thought of that before —

now trains will never be the same
as airplanes

WRAPPING UP

Now it takes both of them,
the fourth-floor couple,
to get the plastic cover around the sun-cot.

The ceremony
mindless of wind
remembers their accomplished style of
comfort, from which sons grown truly gentle
visit but do not persuade them from the precarious
balcony with the plastic sometimes blown half
over the railing.

Last year they shared the evening
paper, passing sections back and forth
in ordered silence.

Now they help each other
up and down, fingers meeting
also to pass the cord one side around the sun-cot,
then the other,
so deep in thought

they do not hear our giggled speculations.
In the night air we outlast them
by another pot of tea
and disapprove of
taking so much trouble on a summer evening.

Indoors our air
has heard it all before, the laundry's
scattered on the bed.

ESSENTIALS

Evening into our separate stupors
falls—I mumble, leave you with
television

Touching by accident we are
polite, lie without
sleeping

three nights unsettling
toward a werewolf hour, we
fierce we
tear each other, cry
essentials
through our claws

and wake still different
creatures, cold but knowing better
where our feet are

Tulips get bigger every year,
though carnivals diminish,
chocolate bars,
apartments when the furniture arrives, but

tulips get bigger every year,
old neighbours in the park remember us
together
and it doesn't seem so strange now,
our old love that came upon us like a season
nor its turning

Side by side, half
peaceful with compromises
and the curling tulips
beautifully dying,

rare days like this we do not conjure
empires,
excuses,
traps for each other

days like this, shy-
eyeing each other,
our old love seems not half so
crippled

Tulips in the park bloom-
burst the colour
of old men's new clothes

Lake against concrete confronts its wall,
that's how to fight,
persistence and joy

soft days between times,
that's how to win,
leisure persistence and joy

TREES GROWING

Young trees in the elbow of the building
show me — new shoots
up from the clump
strengthen, leaf themselves, this summer
staking the air beyond my balcony, eyeing
the third floor

My own height I used to
gauge against the piano, the refrigerator,
measure my faith against
built things enduring

My present balcony
against the changing trees
stays put,
gathers with potted zinnias also a garden of
things relaxing — smells of the crumbling
footstool, ancient
tripod with its black paint flaking crowned with
marigolds, and the oval
table-top, too perfect a wooden oval to
discard, now weathering, all
propped by the solid

concrete that endures
past the leaves' brush-touching, past
the whole season's
blooms, the balcony
measuring itself against their
patient seasonal return

My body, done its growing,
hovers—I measure trees against
my second-floor situation
on the elbow side

Thin trees grow, their function
keeping the building
put

Held watching in a tree-step
season, I am the
still, the
measured-against.

It's not where I'd rather be,
alone under the railway bridge afraid of gravel—
with you efficient and the camera fast and unexpected
as a needle, I look
everywhere else, restore
an ordinary day in which you are,
more realistically,
fat, squat as a buddha on my head, your weight
balances my walk and my brain wish-
hatches at you, even

side by side in a day unfavoured by the sun
and shadows that we needed—
getting the films to the drugstore we are not even
caught in the rain.

Sometimes it works that way
and sometimes not,
days later, my barbed
beak out of your belly and your claw
freshly removed, we remember
on the last of many errands
the photos and returning home do
other things, put on the
kettle, can't decide whether to
wait for each other

then tentatively spread them out together on the bed
and it comes soft-raining back
in 80 photo-pieces of a day you watched me
happy-hatching everywhere I looked, the chance
flowers and the wire fence
large as guests.

TONGUES

Language is what we have—days before
countries, our material baggage
chance or scarce, we carry
precious and preserved our names for
mother, father, fire, water,
home (the gods and vegetables varying
with terrain).

It traps us together
or apart,
you and I, our people buried
Canadian by different routes and generations,
carry with slight regional variations
our now only language
through an age where I is more polite than me,
in actual usage,
coffee more American than tea—
we know the beat words, hip words, words
that read quite well in documenting thickness of Antarctic
ice, and words that designate some vital matters still
four-letter or four-syllable

that kept our people
furtive in an English-speaking land—
inhospitable language ours,
we supplement thee, honour them along,
with splendour of tongue-touches, grunts and song.

Remember the one about the tree
falling in the forest
and the forest so big no-one could hear it—

these days everyone hears
everything,
people on the bus who get off at the usual stop anyway,
all the neighbours, who no longer complain about such things,
and their radios hear me and continue
just the same

but Holland
stops,
together we listen for a
shining
tree-crashing
falling-like-snow
poem.

Large people with small names
the second summer whispers us again

calling my ear a gentler
entrance and persuading to your gentle-freckled
back my hands

with many-petalled names
large-laden

MENDING JEANS

You present your bluejeans
warmer than my hand

I sew delighted the wrong
parts together with large gestures,

panic for the lost
needle with a sly look
as if you are still in the chair, then

catching myself in the act I

sew up the quarter-sized hole in the pocket,
make it better,

just as you rise from the shower, bluejeans
warm and buckle
jingling

Sabbath of alternate small
meals and lover's naps, June
weather I had thought to stretch and catch
my breath into,

and there you are on the edge of a
chair,
reading aloud for the first time,

urgent, eloquent into the long day discovering
how ancient men who dealt in languages and dreams
return from journeys
with wild tales

GIN RUMMY AT 8 PM

Cross-legged on the bed,
our island,
we deal

messages—the cards
curve sure or flutter,
magic-touch their whimsical
marks, or land
flat-backed with coloured
bellies up

We have freed
hours for this—
our untapped childhoods
come into their own,
we slow, we cultivate
our sure, eventual
urgency

and always win
each other, we are always
a surprise

Our gamut of scores
triumphantly or secretly recorded
equal over a week—

discovered on the backs of shopping lists,
crossed off as on the legendary
tree-carved calendars, they testify

our self-made
deserts of time, in which we
loved, were not
alone

COMING HOME, POST-OPERATIVE

A litty titty, oh,
a litty titty, oh,
a litty titty, oh,
and a big titty, too, lookin'

crooked at de hubband,
what de hubband gonna do?

Some of the poems have appeared in Rune and
Tamarack Review, and some have been
broadcast on CBC Anthology.
The author is grateful also to the Canada Council
for assistance in the writing of the book.

Library of Congress Catalogue Card No. 74-31954
ISBN 0 88750 145 1 (hardcover)
ISBN 0 88750 147 8 (softcover)

Edited by Michael Macklem.
Designed and composed at the Dreadnaught press
using Elizabeth capitals and Joanna italic.
Printed in Canada by the Coach House Press.

PUBLISHED IN CANADA BY
OBERON PRESS

By the same author :
No Lingering Peace (Fiddlehead, 1972)